SPACE

30 step-by-step drawing projects inside!

Rob Jensen

Designer Emma Wicks
Senior Production Editor Jennifer Murray
Senior Production Controller Louise Minihane
Senior Acquisitions Editor Pete Jorgensen
Managing Art Editor Jo Connor
Managing Director Mark Searle
Written and Illustrated by Rob Jensen

Designed and Edited by Elizabeth T. Gilbert and Rebecca Razo
at Coffee Cup Creative, LLC.

Copyedited by Beth Adelman

First American Edition, 2025
Published in the United States by DK Publishing
1745 Broadway, 20th Floor, New York, NY 10019

Page design copyright © 2025 Dorling Kindersley Limited
DK, a Division of Penguin Random House LLC
25 26 27 28 10 9 8 7 6 5 4 3 2 1
001-345693-July/2025

© 2025 Art for Kids Hub

All rights reserved.
No part of this publication may be reproduced, stored in or introduced
into a retrieval system, or transmitted, in any form, or by any means
(electronic, mechanical, photocopying, recording, or otherwise), without
the prior written permission of the copyright owner.

No part of this publication may be used or reproduced in any manner for
the purpose of training artificial intelligence technologies or systems. In
accordance with Article 4(3) of the DSM Directive 2019/790, DK expressly
reserves this work from the text and data mining exception.

A catalog record for this book
is available from the Library of Congress.
ISBN 978-0-5939-6444-6

DK books are available at special discounts when purchased
in bulk for sales promotions, premiums, fund-raising, or educational use.
For details, contact: DK Publishing Special Markets,
1745 Broadway, 20th Floor, New York, NY 10019
SpecialSales@dk.com

Printed and bound in China

www.dk.com

www.artforkidshub.com

Draw with ART FOR KIDS HUB

SPACE

30 step-by-step drawing projects inside!

Rob Jensen

Welcome to Art for Kids Hub!........ 6
About This Book........ 7
Art Tools & Supplies........ 8
Getting Started........ 11
All About Color........ 14

PART I: Step-by-Step Projects....16

Earth & Sun Besties........ 18
Solar Eclipse........ 20
Space Kitten........ 22
Our Star, the Sun........ 24
Coming-in-Hot Meteor........ 26
Mars Rover........ 28
Cow Abduction........ 30
Earth's Friend, the Moon........ 32
Mercury & Venus........ 34
Early Astronomer Galileo........ 36
A Singing Satellite........ 38
Super Speedy Rocket........ 40
Flo the Floating Astronaut........ 42
Jolly Jupiter........ 44
Asteroid Buddies........ 46
Hubble Space Telescope........ 48
Black Hole........ 50
Red Planet Landscape........ 52
Apollo the Alien........ 54
Smiley Saturn........ 56
Scientist Albert Einstein........ 58
Uranus & Neptune........ 60
Astronaut Mae Jemison........ 62
Spectacular Shooting Star........ 64

Table of CONTENTS

Dwarf Plant Pluto......................66
Astro the Space Pup..................68
Rocco the Robot......................70
Astronaut Sally Ride..................72
Luna the Lander......................74
Tippy the Tardigrade.................76

PART II: You're an Artist!....78

Symbols...............................78
Speech Bubbles.......................79
Action & Movement..................80
Out-of-This-World Props.............81
Putting It All Together...............86
Folding Surprise Drawings............88
Folding Alien Invasion................90
Earth Day Party......................93

About the Artist......................95
Some Words of Gratitude.............96

Welcome to Art for Kids Hub!

Hey, friends! I'm Rob. And along with my amazing wife, Teryn, and our four creative kids, Jack, Hadley, Austin, and Olivia, we make art together as a family—and we love sharing it with you! Outer space is such a fascinating topic, and we always have lots of fun exploring the universe through drawing.

This book is divided into two parts. In Part I, you'll find step-by-step drawing lessons for a variety of space-themed projects. Each drawing is ranked Level 1, Level 2, or Level 3 according to its difficulty (see the Symbol Key on the opposite page). Don't worry, though! You'll be able to draw all the projects by following along step by step.

In Part II, you'll find tips for drawing backgrounds, props, and completed scenes. I've also included some out-of-this-world folding surprise drawing projects at the very end. Whether you're a beginner or a budding artist, there's something fun for everyone.

Ready to begin? Grab your art tools and some paper, and let's make space art that brings smiles and creates joy!

ROB · AUSTIN · TERYN · JACK · OLIVIA · HADLEY

About This Book

For each project, follow the steps in red to complete your drawing. Then add color using your favorite art tools. It's as simple as that!

Symbol Key

Each project is marked with one of the following symbols, from less difficult to a little more challenging. But don't be afraid to try them all!

 = Level 1

 = Level 2

 = Level 3

 = Great work!

MORE IN THIS BOOK

☑ Draw a jet pack, telescope, space helmet, and other space-themed props.

☑ Combine drawings to make completed scenes.

☑ Create fun folding surprise drawings.

Art Tools & SUPPLIES

Here are some art tools you can use to draw and color the projects in this book. These are some of my favorite supplies, but you can use any tools that are available to you.

Black Marker

I like to draw with a permanent black marker for a bold, solid outline. But feel free to begin your drawings with pencil if you prefer.

Paper

White marker paper is perfect if you're using markers to color, and regular paper is fine if you're using crayons or colored pencils.

CHECKLIST

- ☑ A flat drawing surface, like a table or clipboard
- ☑ Marker paper
- ☑ Black permanent marker
- ☑ Pencil and sharpener
- ☑ Coloring tools, such as colored pencils, markers, and crayons

8

Markers

Markers create smooth, solid strokes of color. Some sets include both fine tips and thick tips. I use alcohol-based markers because they dry quickly, and their colors don't fade easily.

Crayons

Wax crayons are inexpensive and easy to find. Sometimes they create a bumpy texture and can be hard to blend, so I use gel crayons. They are creamy and extra smooth.

Colored Pencils

These tools are clean and simple. You can even layer them to blend and shade. Keep a sharpener on hand for pointy tips.

Pastels

There are two types of pastels: soft pastels and oil pastels. Soft pastels feel like chalk and create smooth, light blends. Oil pastels feel more like crayons and create bold, bright strokes.

We would LOVE to see your drawings! Learn how to share them with us here.

Brushes

Brushes come in a range of sizes and shapes. Brushes with natural bristles are best for watercolor paints, and synthetic bristles are best for acrylics. When you've finished painting, rinse your brushes with soap and warm water, and reshape the bristles before they dry.

Paints

Watercolor, tempera, and acrylic are water-based paints that you can use to color your art. Be sure to use them on sturdy paper, such as watercolor paper. While you paint, keep a cup of water nearby for rinsing your brushes—and have plenty of paper towels on hand for cleanup.

WATERCOLOR

TEMPERA

ACRYLIC

Getting STARTED

Before you begin drawing, it's a great idea to warm up. From dots and swirls to dashes and curls, make all sorts of marks on scrap paper to get the creative juices flowing.

I use a lot of loops, dots, and curvy, squiggly, and jagged lines in my drawings. What other lines and scribbles can you make?

Basic Shapes

Most of the drawings in the book start with basic shapes like circles, triangles, squares, and ovals. Practice drawing these basic shapes and then draw new shapes of your own, if you like.

TRIANGLES

CIRCLES, OVALS & BEAN SHAPES

SQUARES, RECTANGLES & DIAMONDS

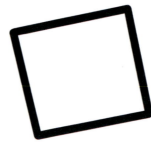
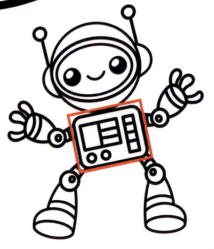

"A happy expression is my favorite, but it's fun to draw other emotions too."

Expressions

The face reveals a character's emotions. In the examples below, see how the eyes, mouth, and other features can help you communicate feelings and personality.

HAPPY

SCARED

SILLY

ANGRY

SNEAKY

TIRED

EMBARRASSED

SWEET

EXCITED

All About COLOR

The Color Wheel

The color wheel is a visual aid for understanding how colors work together. The colors on this wheel are divided into two groups: primary (blue, yellow, red) and secondary (green, orange, purple).

Complementary Colors

Complementary colors are two colors that are opposite each other on the color wheel. When they're placed next to each other in a drawing or painting, they appear brighter. Some examples are yellow and purple, blue and orange, and red and green.

Color Temperature

Colors are divided into two temperatures: cool and warm. Blue, green, and purple are cool colors. Yellow, orange, and red are warm colors. Color temperature plays a part in the mood of a drawing. For example, cool colors are calm and warm colors are energetic.

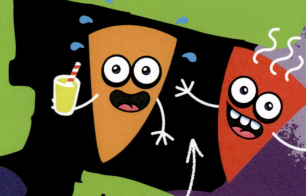

WARM

COOL

Color Mixing

Every color combination begins with the primary colors. Secondary colors are made by mixing two primary colors. Yellow + red = orange, red + blue = purple, and blue + yellow = green. Gray is made by mixing white and black, while pink is made from a combination of white and red. White lightens colors; black darkens colors.

Coloring Steps

To bring your characters to life, try this three-step approach to adding color.

Add smooth, flat areas of color with your tools of choice.

Layer your colors—or use slightly darker shades—to create shadows.

Finish coloring your art by adding highlights with white.

I like to get creative with color in my drawings! How about you?

15

Hey, art friends!

To draw the space-themed projects in this section, start with step 1 and continue to follow each new step in red. Along the way, you'll find lots of encouragement, helpful art tips, and even some fun and interesting facts.

I had so much fun creating these drawing lessons, but we especially love drawing together as a family. So, in addition to my drawings, you'll also see tons of great drawings by Teryn, Jack, Hadley, Austin, and Olivia. Each of us has our own art style, and we want to inspire you to draw in your own unique style, too. There are no mistakes and no wrong ways to make art—the important thing is to have fun and practice!

Happy creating!

Draw two circles. Then add the sun's arm and Earth's eyes.

1

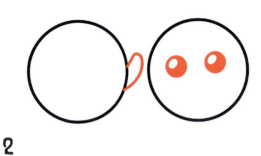

2

Follow the lines in red to draw the faces, sun rays, and land masses.

3

4

Complete the sun's mouth and draw more rays. Finish the continent lines and add a few clouds.

5

6

Excellent work, artists. High five!

Try This!

On a large piece of paper, draw all the planets in the solar system, rotating around the sun. Turn to page 86 to see how.

19

Solar ECLIPSE

Draw a circle for the moon and a backwards C for the sun.

1

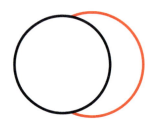
2

Then add the eyes and mouths. Remember that only one eye of the sun is showing!

3

4

Finish the mouths. Then add rays to the sun and craters to the moon.

5

6

DID YOU KNOW?

There are two types of eclipses: solar and lunar. In a solar eclipse, the moon passes directly between the sun and Earth, blocking the sun's light. In a lunar eclipse, Earth's shadow makes the moon appear dark.

20

2

Space KITTEN

DID YOU KNOW?
In 1947, a rocket launched fruit flies out of Earth's atmosphere so scientists could study the effects of radiation on living things, making them the first animals to travel to space.

Begin by drawing the kitten's helmet, face, and torso.

1

2

3

Now begin the ears and legs. Follow the steps in red to develop the helmet and space suit.

4

5

6

Finish with a curved tail and the final details. That's one brave cat!

7

Try This!

Does Mittens need a jet pack or a telescope? Turn to page 83 to draw these and other props!

23

Our Star, THE SUN

Draw a circle and start the sunglasses. Draw two wavy rays.

1

2

Add more rays. Draw rims on the sunglasses and outline the mouth.

3

4

Add more rays, a row of teeth, and a tongue.

5

6

DID YOU KNOW?

From our perspective on Earth, it's hard to imagine how giant and hot our sun is. Scientists say that 1.3 million Earths could fit inside the sun—and they estimate the sun's core to be 27,000,000°F!

24

Start with a round, bumpy shape. Then begin drawing the face.

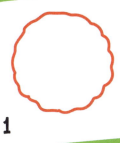

1

2

Finish the mouth and add some texture on the edges.

3

4

Give it a cratered surface and a fiery tail.

5

6

Color your drawing!

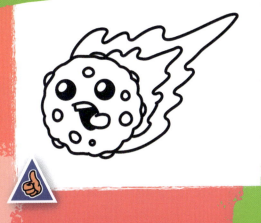

Try This!

Grab a large piece of paper or a poster board. Then draw a variety of meteors in all shapes and sizes. Add a backdrop of sky, if you like, and the landscape below. Now you've got a meteor shower!

3

Mars ROVER

Try This! Create a small fleet of rover friends in a variety of shapes, sizes, and colors.

Start by drawing three wheels.

1

2

3

Then build the body, solar panels, head, and legs.

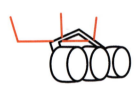
4

5

6

Follow the steps in red to develop the head, wheels, and other details.

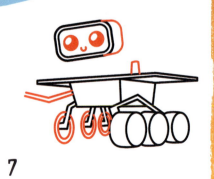
7

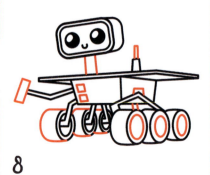
8

9

28

Begin by drawing the cow's face and the bottom of the flying saucer.

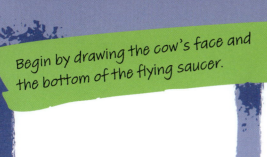

1

2

3

Build the cow's body and the middle of the flying saucer. Add the alien's head.

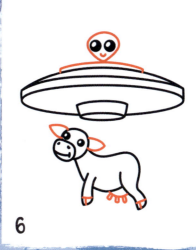

4

5

6

Follow the steps in red to complete the drawing. Don't forget the beam of light!

7

8

31

Earth's Friend, THE MOON

Draw a circle. Then begin the eyes and mouth.

Finish the face and add some large craters.

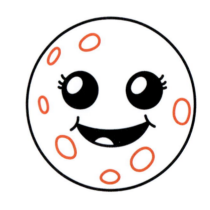

Now draw a handful of smaller craters.

Mercury & VENUS

You can see Venus and Mercury in the sky just before sunrise and just after sunset. Venus is bright—just like my drawing.

I colored my Mercury light blue. I love his friendly wink!

Draw two circles, leaving a gap in each one for the arms.

1

2

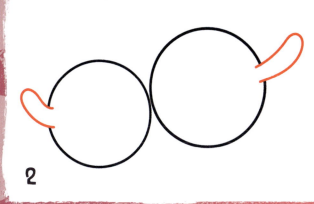

Add another arm on each planet. Then draw the faces.

3

4

Draw circles for craters on Mercury. Finish Venus with swirls of clouds.

5

DID YOU KNOW?

Mercury is closer to the sun than any other planet in our solar system, but Venus is hotter. The thick atmosphere on Venus is full of carbon dioxide, which traps the sun's heat and results in a surface temperature of 870°F!

Draw Galileo's eyes, nose, mustache, cheeks, and eyebrows.

1

2

3

Add the beard. Then begin drawing the body and telescope.

4

5

6

Follow the simple steps in red to continue.

7

8

Now finish the hair and telescope details. Add his legs and feet.

9

DID YOU KNOW?

Often called "the father of astronomy," Galileo was an Italian who lived in the 1600s. He designed and used his own telescope to observe the night sky. This led him to many celestial discoveries, including the four largest moons of Jupiter, the rings of Saturn, and sunspots.

A Singing SATELLITE

I gave my satellite a big mouth to show it singing as it soars through space.

Satellites travel around 17,000 miles per hour. No wonder mine looks frightened!

Draw one circle. Then draw a smaller circle inside, as shown.

1

2

Next, draw the face. Then add two square panels.

3

4

Add the antenna, face details, and a grid pattern to the panels.

5

6

Excellent work, space artists!

DID YOU KNOW?

The word "satellite" refers to any object that orbits a larger body. The many satellites currently orbiting the Earth serve a variety of functions, including providing phone and Internet service, predicting weather patterns, and showing locations on maps.

39

Super Speedy ROCKET

DID YOU KNOW? Rockets are thrust into space using a chemical reaction. Rocket propellant is a combination of fuel (such as liquid hydrogen) and an oxidizer (such as liquid oxygen) that is ignited at liftoff.

Draw a leaf shape for the body. Then add fins, boosters, and stripes.

1

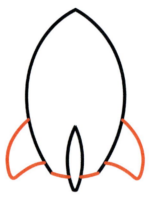
2

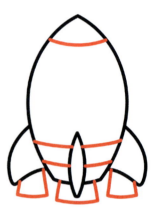
3

Draw the window, stripes on the boosters, and fiery flames. Don't forget the face!

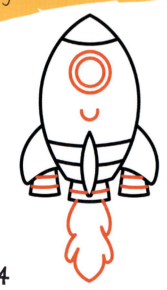
4

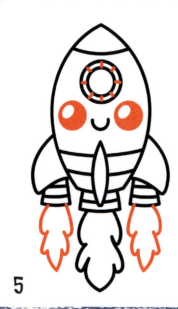
5

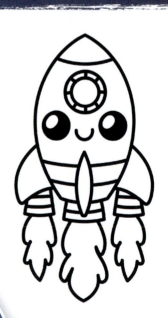

40

2
Flo the Floating ASTRONAUT

Jack, what's an astronaut's favorite snack? A Milky Way!

DID YOU KNOW?
When in zero gravity, the human spine gets longer. Astronauts temporarily "grow" about 3 percent taller while in space.

Ha! What's an astronaut's favorite drink? Gravi-tea.

Begin by drawing the helmet, face, and head.

1

2

3

Add the ears, body, and hair. Detail the space suit with stripes, patches, and buttons.

4

5

6

Now draw gloves and boots. Add a few finishing touches to the suit and helmet.

7

Try This!

Now that you've learned how, draw your next astronaut floating upside-down!

43

Draw a circle with a face. Then outline Jupiter's red spot.

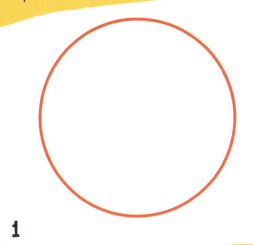

Fill in the mouth and use wavy lines to draw cloud bands across the face.

Excellent work. That's one jolly giant!

DID YOU KNOW?
Jupiter's Great Red Spot is a giant storm caused by an area of extremely high pressure in the atmosphere. The storm is larger than Earth, although it has been slowly shrinking over time. NASA believes this storm has been raging for at least 300 years!

Asteroid BUDDIES

Outline the group of asteroids and begin drawing their faces.

1

2

Add some playful expressions along with some eyelashes, if you'd like!

3

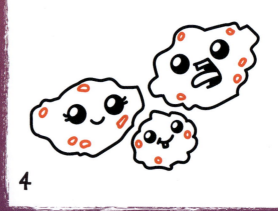

4

Add a few bumpy cracks on each asteroid to complete your drawing.

5

Hubble Space TELESCOPE

Start the telescope by drawing a simple cylinder. Then begin the face.

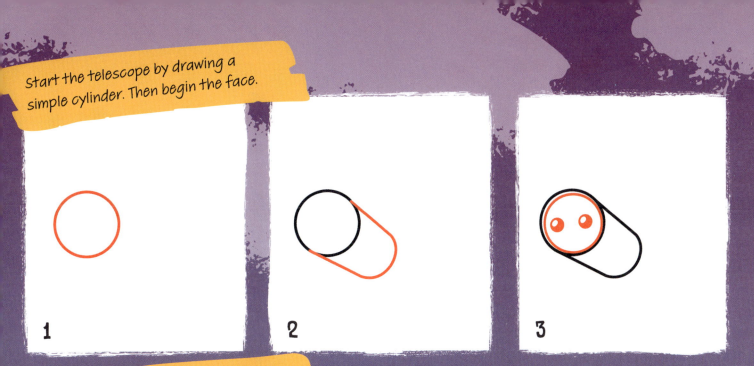

Follow the steps in red to build the body, panels, and antennae.

Draw a flap above the face (called the aperture door) and finish with just a few more details.

DID YOU KNOW?

Launched in 1990, the Hubble Space Telescope orbits Earth about 320 miles above the surface. It transmits images to us from beyond the Earth's atmosphere, providing clearer pictures of space than ever before!

49

Begin with a half circle as you draw the top and middle of the black hole.

1

2

Add the eyes, the bottom half of the circle, and a tall mouth. Then outline the light bending around the hole.

3

4

To complete the black hole, add another layer of bending light. Looks awesome!

5

Try This!

Black holes can tear apart planets, stars, and other celestial bodies that come too close. Add some objects to the scene that are trying to make an escape!

3
Red Planet LANDSCAPE

Begin by drawing an alien creature and some plant-like forms on the ground.

1

Add the horizon and a few rocky structures in the distance. Begin the flying saucer.

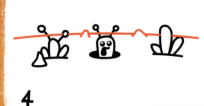
4

5

6

Finish the saucer. Add a sun, a moon, craters, and other fun details.

7

8

Apollo the ALIEN

DID YOU KNOW?
The acronym "UFO" stands for "unidentified flying object." Most UFO sightings turn out to be meteors, human-made aircraft, weather balloons, or even birds, but it can be fun to wonder!

Draw the alien's nostrils, smiling mouth, and large eyes.

1

2

Add the round head, eyebrows, antennae, and body. Begin drawing the flying saucer.

3

4

Try This!

UFOs are often imagined as flying saucers, but they can be any shape. Try drawing triangular, square, and hexagonal ships for your alien!

Follow the steps in red to finish the antennae, legs, arms, and saucer.

5

6

54

Smiley SATURN

DID YOU KNOW? Saturn is known for its dense rings, which are made up of ice, rocks, and dust. The rings are more than twice as wide as Saturn itself!

Saturn has 146 moons—the most of any planet in our solar system!

That's right! Its largest moon is Titan. I think I'll add that to my drawing.

Draw part of a circle and a tilted inner ring. Then add the eyes and mouth.

1

2

Finish the mouth and add the rest of the planet's rings.

3

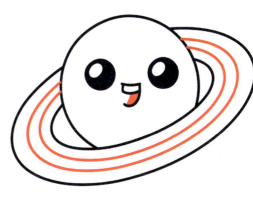
4

To finish, add curved lines across the face. Looks great!

5

57

② Scientist ALBERT EINSTEIN

DID YOU KNOW?
Albert Einstein was a famous scientist who developed the theory of relativity, changing the way we think about gravity. His theory led to the discovery of black holes and the idea that our universe is expanding. What a smart guy!

To give his crazy hair some dimension, I added shadows with gray markers.

I gave Einstein a pin-striped vest and pants with a brown jacket. He's lookin' sharp!

Begin by drawing the face, head, and torso. Add the top of the mustache.

1

2

3

Add details to the torso and complete his face. Then draw the wild mop of hair!

4

5

6

Finish by adding the arms, legs, hands, and feet. Nice work!

7

8

59

Uranus & NEPTUNE

Neptune is known for its deep blue color, and Uranus is blue-green due to methane gas in its atmosphere.

DID YOU KNOW?
Just like fellow gas giants Jupiter and Saturn, Uranus and Neptune have rings. The rings of Uranus are nearly vertical because the planet spins on its side, likely due to a collision with a large object long ago.

The distant stars look like sparkles, giving this portrait a magical touch.

Draw a circle for Neptune and a partial circle for Uranus.

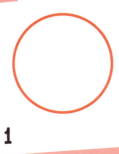

1

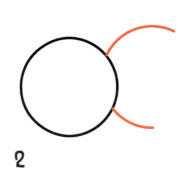

2

Now add rings and a face to Uranus. Complete the circle under the rings.

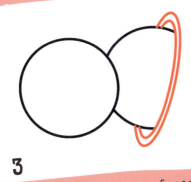

3

4

Follow the steps in red to draw the faces. Add markings on Neptune and a few distant stars in the background.

5

6

Great job! Now you can add some color.

Try This!

Try giving your planets a different combination of expressions. See page 13 for inspiration!

Astronaut MAE JEMISON

Begin by drawing the face, head, and collar.

1

2

3

Follow the steps in red to finish the face, draw the helmet, and begin the body.

4

5

6

Draw the hair and finish the space suit.

7

8

9

Spectacular SHOOTING STAR

"I shaded the edges of my gold star with orange to make it pop from the paper."

"I loved making the rainbow trail! Next time I'll make a meteor shower by drawing a group of shooting stars."

Draw the shape of the star with rounded tips.

Add a swirling trail using curved lines. Then add the face.

Complete the trail with another swirl. Then add eyelashes, if you'd like!

DID YOU KNOW?
Shooting (or falling) stars aren't actually stars at all. They are meteors made of rock and dust that burn up after entering Earth's atmosphere, appearing to glow as they streak across the sky.

Dwarf Planet PLUTO

Draw a circle. Then add the face and arms.

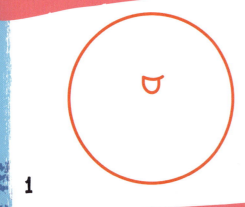
1

2

Now draw the heart and its face.

3

4

Add a few circles for craters. Well done!

5

Draw a circle for the helmet. Then add the face and ears.

1

2

3

Finish the head and build the helmet and body.

4

5

6

Develop the helmet, body, and space suit.

7

8

Add an antenna, tail, paws, and space suit details. He's ready to fly!

9

DID YOU KNOW?
In 1960, two female dogs named Belka and Strelka were sent into space on the Soviet spacecraft Sputnik 5. They were the first living creatures to return safely after orbiting Earth.

69

3

Rocco the ROBOT

Try This!

Accessorize your robot with wires, tools, gears, or wheels. See pages 81–85 for more prop ideas and fun extras.

Draw a circle with a face. Then add a rectangle for the body.

1

2

Add a small circle for each limb joint. Use two ovals for the opening in the helmet.

3

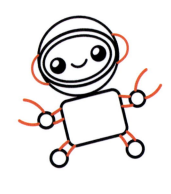

4

Follow the steps in red to build the antennae, control board, and limbs.

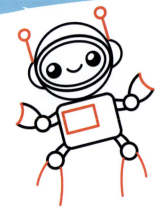

5

6

Astronaut SALLY RIDE

Begin by drawing the face, head, hairline, and collar.

1

2

3

Add the hair and torso. Then begin drawing the helmet and limbs.

4

5

6

Finish by drawing hands, boots, and uniform details.

7

8

3

Luna the LANDER

Austin, I love how your lander looks like a robotic spider!

Try This!

Gray, silver, orange, and gold are great for coloring metal objects. But you can try any colors you'd like!

Don't forget to share your lunar lander with us!

74

Begin by drawing the body, two legs, and a squished octagon for the head.

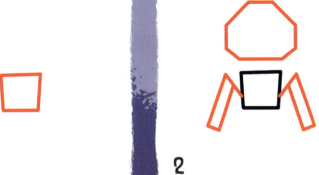

1 2 3

Follow the steps in red to draw the eyes. Continue building the module.

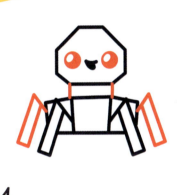
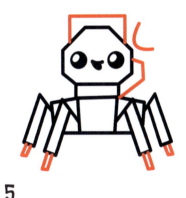

4 5 6

Finish the details, such as the rungs of the ladder and bottoms of the feet.

7

DID YOU KNOW?

A lunar lander is a spacecraft designed to touch down softly on the moon's surface. The most famous lunar lander in history is the Apollo Lunar Module (named Eagle), which carried the first astronauts to ever walk on the moon.

75

Tippy the TARDIGRADE

Draw this creature's head and chubby body. Begin adding spiky claws to the limbs.

1

2

3

Continue adding rounded segments and limbs to the body.

4

5

6

Complete the limbs and claws.

7

8

Part II: YOU'RE AN ARTIST!

In this section, you'll learn how to draw things that add interest to your art. I've also included instructions for creating two folding surprise drawings. Remember, there are no mistakes—your only goal is to have fun!

Symbols

Symbols can be used to express emotions, feelings, movement, or a state of mind. For example, replacing a character's eyes with stars suggests they might be daydreaming about the cosmos. Drawing swirly lines behind a character can make them appear to float. What other symbols could you add to your drawings?

SPARKLES
Use sparkles to show distant stars or shimmering light.

DASHES
Dotted and dashed lines with an aircraft, such as a spaceship, can show lift-off or flight.

STARS & LINES
Stars and lines can help suggest fast-moving celestial objects, such as the whoosh of a comet or meteor.

Speech Bubbles

Add personality to your characters with speech bubbles that show what they're saying or thinking.

Round and rectangular speech bubbles give your characters the ability to "talk" to each other or your readers.

This speech bubble is used to express enthusiasm or excitement!

This thought cloud reveals a character's internal thoughts to the reader.

What Austin said.

Action & Movement

These fun details can add interest to your space drawings by showing them in action and bringing them to life.

HOVERING
Draw wavy lines under an object to show that it's hovering.

ORBITING
Show an object's orbit using dashed lines.

ZOOMING
Show an object's speed by trailing it with straight, parallel lines.

GLOWING
Loosely outline your characters to make them glow—this works best with bright colors!

BLASTING
Draw cloud shapes for a blast of smoke.

EXPLODING
Zigzagged lines with sharp points suggest a powerful explosion.

Out-of-This-World PROPS

Props are objects that add character, style, and a sense of place to your drawings. Rockets are excellent space props!

Rocket & Spaceship

Use rectangles, triangles, and even arrowhead shapes to create rockets and spaceships. The possibilities are endless! Don't forget to add stripes, fins, and flames.

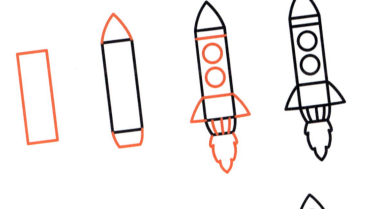
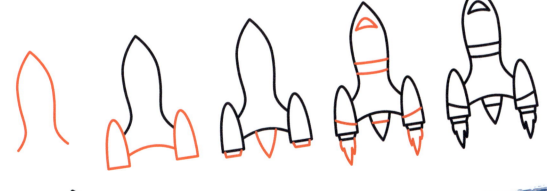

I love imagining what it's like to be in space, surrounded by cool technology and awesome celestial scenes. In addition to the props I've drawn, what other space-themed objects can you think up to draw?

Command Center

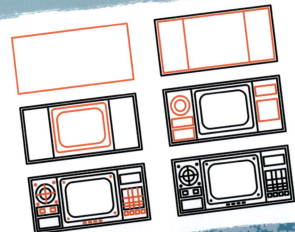

Draw a rectangle for the console. Then add panels, screens, and buttons.

Space Helmet

Draw a circle. Then add the mask, a camera, and an antenna.

Navigation Beacon

Draw an upside-down cup and base. Add an antenna and details to suggest a radio signal.

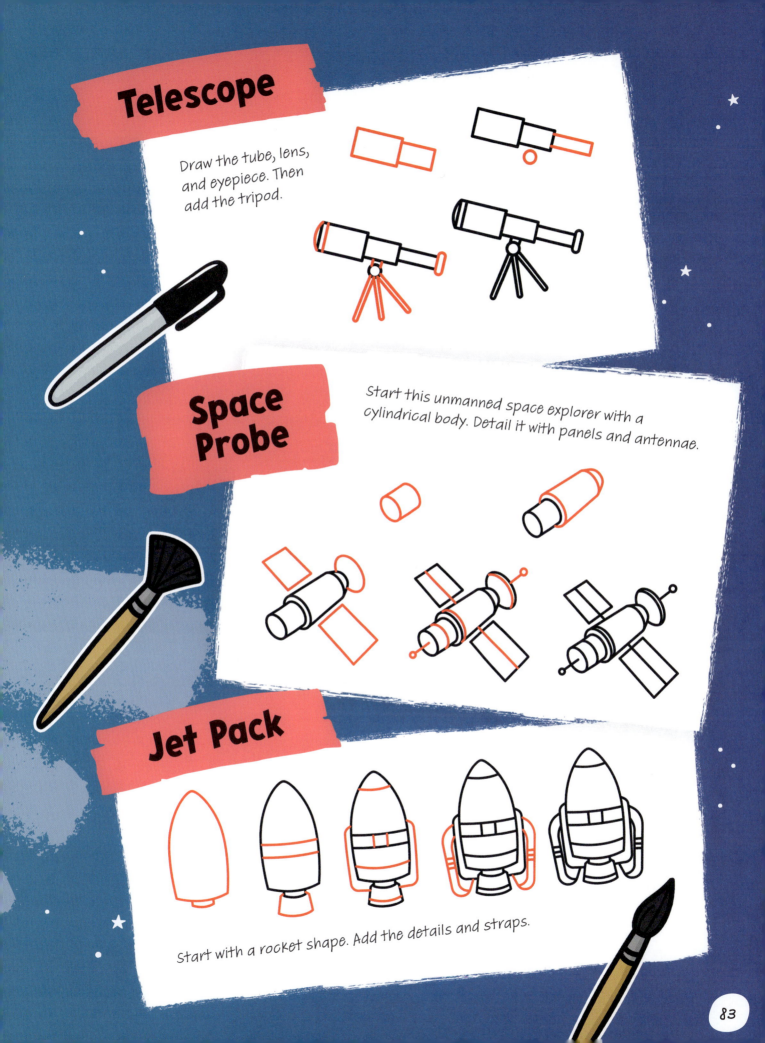

Asteroids & Meteors

Draw some wobbly rocks with craters in various sizes. Add more stars, pebbles, and lines to show movement, if you like.

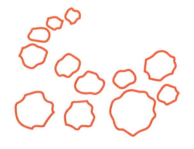
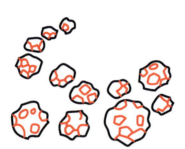

Try this style!

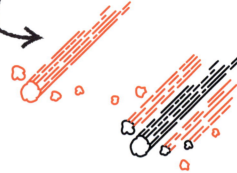

Space Crystals

Draw pointed crystals in different sizes. Complete the details.

Spiral Galaxy

Draw a C shape for the center. Use curved lines for the swirls and dots for stars.

Nebula

Draw groups of curved, parallel lines. Add sparkles and dots for the stardust.

Wormhole

Follow the steps in red to draw a swirly wormhole.

85

Putting It ALL TOGETHER

Solar System

Folding SURPRISE DRAWINGS

A folding surprise drawing is exactly what it sounds like: a drawing on folded paper that opens to reveal a surprise inside! This project is a lot of fun and gives you an opportunity to stretch your creativity.

Before you begin, you'll need to prepare your paper so the surprise works the way it should. I used a sheet of printer paper (8.5" x 11"), but you can use any size paper you like.

Paper Set Up

1. Lay the paper flat with the short sides of the paper on the top and bottom, and the long sides of the paper on the left and right. Fold the paper in half, lining up the top edge with the bottom edge.

2. Press along the fold to make a crease.

3. Gently lift the top flap of the paper.

4. Fold the top flap up, bringing the bottom edge to line up with the top edge. Press along the fold to make another crease.

5. and 6. Lift the paper and flip it over from right to left, so that the unfolded bottom flap is now on the top.

7. Lift the flap and fold it up to meet the top edge, repeating step 4.

8. Open the last fold you just made.

9. Flip your paper over from left to right, so it's back to the original side.

10. Your paper is now ready for your drawing! You will start the outside drawing on the folded paper.

Note: When you unfold the page, you should have four sections marked by folds.

Turn the page to get started on the first surprise drawing!

3
FOLDING ALIEN INVASION

FOLDED

1. Place the paper with the folded side up (see step 10 on page 89). Draw a line above the fold line, then connect each end to the fold.

2. Now add the bottom section of the flying saucer, connecting the lines along the fold.

3. Follow the lines in red to add horizontal sections to the flying saucer.

4. Draw a half circle for the top. Then add a rounded bottom with two short legs.

5. Detail the underside, and then add seams and rivets to the saucer's body.

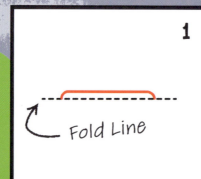
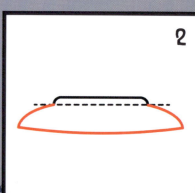
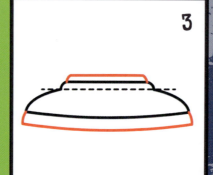
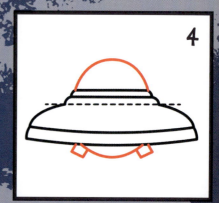
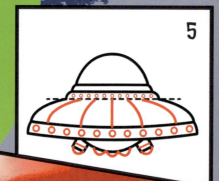
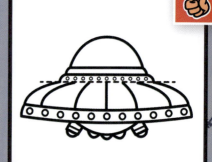

90

OPENED

1. Draw horizontal lines along the top and bottom fold lines.

2. Now add several latches and a few alien heads.

3. Draw the aliens' faces and bodies.

4. Then add their antennae and limbs. Finish with dashed lines to show that they're floating!

Turn the page to see how I colored this scene.

1

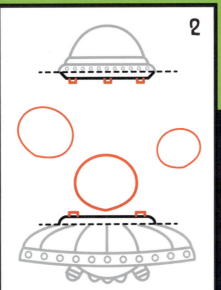
2

3

4

91

COLOR YOUR DRAWING

Add color with the art tools of your choice. I used lime green for the aliens, red for the antennae, gray for the metal saucer, and blue for the window. Then I used a variety of colors for the lights!

Earth Day PARTY

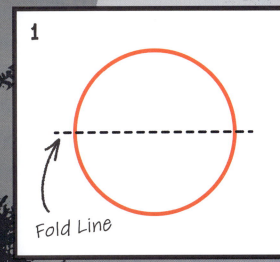
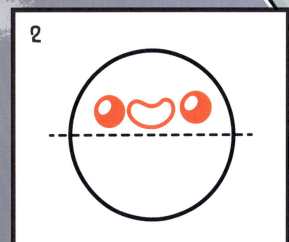
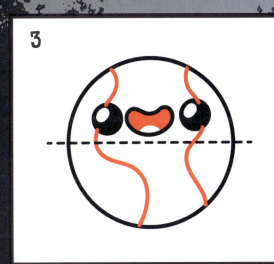

FOLDED

1. Place the paper with the folded side up (see step 10 on page 89). Draw a circle, making half above the fold and half below.

2. Draw the eyes and mouth above the fold line.

3. Color in the mouth, working around the tongue. Then add wavy lines to show land masses.

OPENED

1. Unfold your paper so Earth is split.

2. Now draw a heart in the center.

3. Draw a line along the top fold, connecting to each end of the top half circle. Extend the lines of the bottom half circle above the bottom fold. Then add a face to the heart.

4. Add arms to the heart and fill in the mouth, working around the tongue. Draw oval shapes to show the Earth's core.

5. Use two lines to connect the pieces of the drawing. Then add the sun and moon next to the heart.

Don't forget to color in your drawing. How about adding some fireworks or falling stars to the scene?

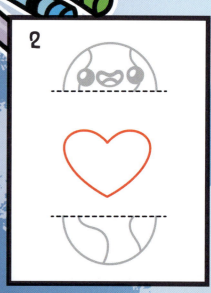
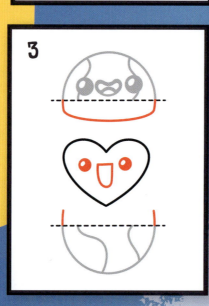
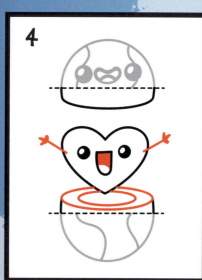
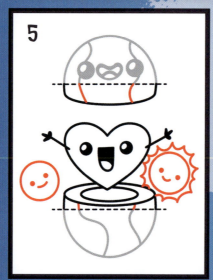

ABOUT THE ARTIST

Rob Jensen, the fun-loving creator of Art for Kids Hub, has a background in industrial design, which fuels his passion for teaching art. He believes that creativity adds happiness and interest to life. Rob, along with his family, embodies the spirit of making art both easy and exciting. Collectively, the Jensens demonstrate that art is not just a solo journey but a shared family adventure. Together, they show the world how to create art in simple, engaging ways, one drawing at a time.

ABOUT ART FOR KIDS HUB

Art for Kids Hub is a family-driven platform that brings the joy of art to families around the world. Co-created by Rob Jensen and his family, it offers a friendly, welcoming space for kids of all ages to learn and grow artistically. Recognized by various media outlets, Art for Kids Hub provides a diverse range of resources, including an engaging website, an online shop, and social media content full of art lessons. This platform is committed to making learning art fun and accessible, showcasing that art can be a delightful experience for everyone. It complements traditional art teaching by adding its unique, family-oriented touch. Visit artforkidshub.com.

SOME WORDS OF GRATITUDE

In the creation of this book, I've been surrounded by an incredible circle of support and inspiration, each person contributing uniquely to this journey.

To Teryn, my wife and partner in everything: Your love, support, and friendship are the cornerstones of not only this book but of all our endeavors. I am endlessly grateful for your presence in my life. You make everything possible.

My deepest gratitude also goes to our children—Jack, Hadley, Austin, and Olivia. Your creativity, laughter, and shared joy in art have been the foundation of not only this book but all we do at Art for Kids Hub. You are my heart and inspiration.

A heartfelt thank you to DK, my publisher, for believing in this project. Pete Jorgensen, who first reached out to me with this wonderful opportunity: Your confidence in my work has been a great honor. Working with DK has been an enriching and fulfilling experience.

Special appreciation goes to Rebecca Razo and Elizabeth Gilbert at Coffee Cup Creative, LLC. Your expertise and vision have been instrumental in bringing this book to life. Your dedication and skill have transformed my ideas into something tangible and beautiful.

To my parents, Greg and Ruth Jensen, thank you for your unwavering encouragement and support since my childhood. Your belief in my passion for drawing has been a guiding light throughout my life and career.

I am also profoundly grateful to the young artists and their families who have joined us on Art for Kids Hub. Your enthusiasm and creativity have been a continuous source of inspiration and joy.

To the broader community of educators, fellow artists, and supporters, thank you for your encouragement and invaluable feedback. You have helped foster a nurturing space for young artists to thrive.

This book is a tribute to all of you. Your support, in so many ways, has made this journey an enriching and joyous adventure. Thank you for being part of our art family!

Rob Jensen